Teamwork Triumph: Mastering Leadership in Every Setting

Mary Smith

Copyright © [2023]

Title: Teamwork Triumph: Mastering Leadership in Every Setting

Author's: Mary Smith

All rights reserved. No part of this publication may be reproduced, stored in a retrieval system, or transmitted in any form or by any means, electronic, mechanical, photocopying, recording, or otherwise, without the prior written permission of the publisher or author, except in the case of brief quotations embodied in critical reviews and certain other non-commercial uses permitted by copyright law.

This book was printed and published by [Publisher's: **Mary Smith**] in [2023]

ISBN:

TABLE OF CONTENT

Chapter 1: Introduction to Teamwork and Leadership — 07

The Importance of Teamwork in Today's World

The Role of Leadership in Team Environments

Understanding the Audience: Who Can Benefit from Mastering Leadership?

Chapter 2: Building a Strong Foundation — 13

Developing a Clear Vision and Mission

Defining Roles and Responsibilities

Establishing Effective Communication Channels

Chapter 3: Fostering a Positive Team Culture — 19

Creating a Supportive and Inclusive Environment

Encouraging Collaboration and Cooperation

Celebrating Diversity and Individual Strengths

Chapter 4: Effective Leadership Strategies — 25

Leading by Example

Setting Realistic Goals and Expectations

Motivating and Inspiring Team Members

Chapter 5: Developing Essential Leadership Skills — 31

Effective Communication Techniques

Active Listening and Feedback

Conflict Resolution and Problem Solving

Chapter 6: Empowering and Delegating — 37

Trusting and Empowering Team Members

Delegating Tasks and Responsibilities

Providing Support and Resources

Chapter 7: Leading Through Change and Challenges   43

Adapting to Change and Embracing Innovation

Managing Conflict and Overcoming Obstacles

Learning from Failures and Turning Them into Opportunities

Chapter 8: Inspiring and Motivating Teams   49

Recognizing and Appreciating Team Achievements

Implementing Effective Rewards and Incentives

Creating a Culture of Continuous Learning and Growth

Chapter 9: Leading Cross-Functional and Virtual Teams   55

Strategies for Leading Cross-Functional Teams

Overcoming Challenges in Virtual Team Environments

Leveraging Technology for Effective Communication and Collaboration

Chapter 10: Sustaining High-Performing Teams   62

Building Trust and Cohesion

Promoting Work-Life Balance and Well-being

Nurturing a Culture of Continuous Improvement

Chapter 11: Leadership Beyond the Team   68

Influencing and Inspiring Others Outside the Team

Collaborating with Other Leaders for Organizational Success

Leaving a Legacy: Developing Future Leaders

Chapter 12: Conclusion: Mastering Leadership in Every Setting   74

Reflecting on the Journey

Applying Leadership Skills in Personal and Professional Life

Inspiring Others to Embrace Leadership and Teamwork

Chapter 1: Introduction to Teamwork and Leadership

The Importance of Teamwork in Today's World

In today's fast-paced and interconnected world, the significance of teamwork cannot be overstated. Whether it is in the workplace, sports, or any other setting, the ability to work effectively as a team is essential for success. "Teamwork Triumph: Mastering Leadership in Every Setting" explores the nuances of teamwork and provides valuable insights on how to harness its power.

In today's highly competitive environment, organizations are increasingly recognizing the importance of teamwork. The complex challenges we face require diverse perspectives, skills, and experiences. By working together, teams can leverage their collective strengths, generating innovative solutions and achieving goals that would be impossible to accomplish individually.

Teamwork fosters collaboration, trust, and mutual respect among team members. It encourages open communication and the sharing of ideas, which leads to enhanced problem-solving and decision-making. When individuals feel valued and part of a team, they are more motivated, engaged, and committed to achieving shared objectives.

The book delves into various aspects of teamwork, emphasizing the key elements that contribute to its success. It explores the importance of clearly defined roles and responsibilities, effective communication, and the ability to manage conflicts constructively. It also highlights the significance of strong leadership in fostering a cohesive and high-performing team.

Moreover, "Teamwork Triumph" addresses the challenges that teams may encounter and provides strategies for overcoming them. It discusses how to navigate cultural differences, build trust in virtual teams, and promote inclusivity. The book also emphasizes the importance of celebrating successes and recognizing individual contributions, as these factors contribute to the overall team morale and motivation.

In addition to the workplace, the principles of teamwork explored in this book are applicable to various other settings. Sports teams, community organizations, and even families can benefit from the lessons learned in "Teamwork Triumph." By understanding the dynamics of effective teamwork, individuals can enhance their personal relationships and contribute to the success of their communities.

In conclusion, teamwork is crucial in today's world, where collaboration and innovation are the driving forces behind success. "Teamwork Triumph: Mastering Leadership in Every Setting" serves as a comprehensive guide, providing valuable insights and practical strategies for individuals and teams to unlock their full potential. Whether you are a leader, team member, or someone interested in personal growth, this book is an invaluable resource for mastering the art of teamwork.

The Role of Leadership in Team Environments

In today's dynamic and fast-paced world, teamwork has become an essential component of success in virtually every setting. Whether it's in the corporate world, sports, community organizations, or even within families, the ability to work effectively as a team is crucial. However, the success of any team heavily relies on strong leadership. In this subchapter, we will explore the vital role that leadership plays in team environments and how it can contribute to achieving triumph in every setting.

Leadership is the driving force behind any successful team. It provides guidance, direction, and motivation to the individuals working together towards a common goal. A good leader possesses a combination of skills and qualities that allow them to effectively manage and inspire their team members. They are responsible for creating a positive and cohesive team environment where individuals feel valued and motivated to give their best.

One of the primary responsibilities of a leader in a team environment is to set clear goals and objectives. By clearly defining what needs to be accomplished and the desired outcomes, leaders provide a roadmap for their team members. This helps to align everyone's efforts towards a common purpose, ensuring that the team stays focused and productive.

Moreover, leadership plays a crucial role in fostering effective communication within a team. A leader must encourage open and honest communication among team members, creating an environment where ideas and concerns can be freely shared. This enables better collaboration, problem-solving, and decision-making, ultimately leading to improved team performance.

A leader also serves as a role model for the team. Their behavior and actions set the tone for the entire group. A good leader leads by example, demonstrating integrity, accountability, and professionalism. This inspires team members to follow suit, creating a culture of excellence and high standards within the team.

Furthermore, leadership is essential in managing conflicts and resolving any issues that may arise within a team. Conflicts are inevitable when individuals with different backgrounds, skills, and perspectives come together. A leader must possess conflict resolution skills to address disagreements and ensure that they are resolved in a fair and constructive manner, without damaging team dynamics.

In conclusion, leadership is a fundamental aspect of teamwork in every setting. Effective leadership sets the tone for the team, establishes clear goals, fosters communication, and manages conflicts. By embodying these qualities, a leader can create a positive and productive team environment where individuals can thrive and triumph in their collective endeavors. Whether you are a team member or aspiring to be a leader, understanding the role of leadership in team environments is crucial for success.

Understanding the Audience: Who Can Benefit from Mastering Leadership?

In today's fast-paced and interconnected world, effective leadership is crucial in every setting. Whether you are leading a small team, managing a large organization, or even coordinating a group project, mastering the art of leadership is essential for success. This subchapter aims to help you understand the audience that can benefit from developing leadership skills and how they can apply them in the context of teamwork.

When we talk about the audience that can benefit from mastering leadership, we are referring to everyone. Leadership skills are not limited to a specific profession, industry, or hierarchical position. They are applicable to individuals from all walks of life who engage in teamwork, collaboration, and cooperation.

First and foremost, professionals in the corporate world can greatly benefit from mastering leadership. Whether you are a manager, team leader, or an employee working as part of a team, leadership skills can enhance your ability to communicate effectively, foster a positive work environment, and motivate your team members towards achieving common goals. By understanding the audience and adapting your leadership style accordingly, you can build strong, cohesive teams that consistently deliver outstanding results.

Beyond the corporate world, individuals involved in community organizations, non-profit initiatives, and social causes can also benefit from mastering leadership. These settings often require individuals to work together towards a common purpose, and effective leadership can inspire unity, engage volunteers, and drive positive change.

Additionally, students and educators can also benefit from mastering leadership skills. In educational settings, leadership is not limited to teachers or administrators. Students can develop their own leadership skills by taking initiative, collaborating with peers, and taking on leadership roles within student organizations or group projects. Educators, on the other hand, can use leadership strategies to create a positive and supportive learning environment, fostering student engagement and success.

Ultimately, mastering leadership is not about a specific job title or position; it is about developing essential skills that can be applied in any collaborative setting. By understanding the audience, recognizing their needs, and adapting our leadership style accordingly, we can unlock the full potential of teamwork and achieve remarkable success in every setting.

In the following chapters of "Teamwork Triumph: Mastering Leadership in Every Setting," we will dive deeper into the specific strategies and techniques that can help you develop your leadership skills, empower your team, and create a culture of success. Whether you are a seasoned leader or just starting your journey, this book will provide you with the tools and insights necessary to become a masterful leader in the context of teamwork.

Chapter 2: Building a Strong Foundation

Developing a Clear Vision and Mission

In today's fast-paced and ever-changing world, teamwork has become an essential skill in every setting. Whether you are a business leader, a student, or a member of a community organization, the ability to work effectively with others towards a common goal is crucial for success. However, achieving true teamwork requires more than just getting a group of individuals together. It requires a clear vision and mission that aligns everyone's efforts and drives them towards a shared purpose.

A clear vision provides direction and gives the team a sense of purpose. It answers the question, "What do we want to achieve?" A vision should be inspiring, compelling, and resonate with every member of the team. It should be ambitious enough to motivate and challenge them, yet realistic enough to be achievable. When a team has a clear vision, they can focus their energy and resources towards a common goal, leading to increased productivity and engagement.

A mission, on the other hand, outlines the team's purpose and defines how they will achieve their vision. It answers the question, "How will we achieve our goals?" A mission statement should be concise and specific, outlining the team's core values, objectives, and strategies. It serves as a guiding force, helping team members make decisions and prioritize their actions. A well-defined mission statement ensures that everyone is on the same page and working towards the same end result.

Developing a clear vision and mission requires collaboration and input from every team member. It is important to involve everyone in the process to ensure buy-in and commitment. Encourage open and honest communication, and create a safe space for ideas and opinions to be shared. By involving everyone in the vision and mission development, you create a sense of ownership and accountability, fostering a stronger commitment to the team's goals.

Once a vision and mission are established, it is crucial to consistently communicate and reinforce them. Regularly remind the team of their purpose and how their work contributes to the overall vision. Celebrate milestones and achievements along the way to keep morale high and motivation strong. Constantly evaluate and reassess the vision and mission to ensure they remain relevant and aligned with the team's evolving needs and aspirations.

In conclusion, developing a clear vision and mission is essential for effective teamwork. It provides direction, purpose, and alignment, enabling individuals to work together towards a common goal. By involving every team member in the process and consistently communicating and reinforcing the vision and mission, you can create a strong and united team that can triumph in any setting.

Defining Roles and Responsibilities

In the realm of teamwork, one of the key factors that contribute to success is the clear definition of roles and responsibilities. When every individual understands their specific tasks and obligations within the team, it becomes easier to collaborate effectively and achieve common goals. This subchapter aims to explore the importance of defining roles and responsibilities in various settings, whether it be in a professional environment, sports team, or community group. By mastering this aspect of leadership, individuals can significantly enhance their teamwork abilities and maximize their collective potential.

First and foremost, defining roles and responsibilities helps to establish a sense of clarity and direction within a team. When everyone is aware of their unique contributions, it reduces confusion and ambiguity, streamlining the decision-making process. This clarity fosters a more efficient workflow and minimizes the chances of duplication or gaps in tasks. Additionally, by clearly defining roles, teams can optimize their performance by assigning responsibilities to individuals based on their strengths, skills, and expertise. This not only increases productivity but also boosts morale as members can excel in areas they are best suited for.

Moreover, role definition encourages accountability and fosters a culture of ownership within the team. When individuals understand their responsibilities, they are more likely to take ownership of their tasks, ensuring that they are completed to the best of their abilities. This mindset not only promotes a higher level of commitment but also instills a sense of pride and accomplishment as team members witness the direct impact of their contributions.

Furthermore, clearly defined roles and responsibilities enable effective collaboration and communication among team members. When everyone knows their specific duties, it becomes easier to delegate tasks, coordinate efforts, and share information. This enhances overall coordination and cooperation, leading to improved problem-solving and decision-making processes. Additionally, it reduces conflicts and misunderstandings that may arise due to overlapping responsibilities or lack of clarity.

In conclusion, defining roles and responsibilities is a crucial element in mastering leadership and achieving success in any teamwork setting. It establishes clarity, promotes accountability, encourages ownership, and facilitates effective collaboration. By understanding the significance of role definition and actively working towards implementing it within teams, individuals can unlock their full potential and triumph in their collective endeavors.

Establishing Effective Communication Channels

Communication is the cornerstone of successful teamwork. Without clear and effective channels of communication, teams can quickly become disorganized, inefficient, and ultimately fail to achieve their goals. In this subchapter, we will explore the importance of establishing effective communication channels in any team setting and provide practical strategies for improving communication among team members.

Effective communication is essential for fostering collaboration, sharing ideas, and ensuring that everyone is on the same page. When communication channels are established and utilized efficiently, teams can overcome challenges, make informed decisions, and achieve their objectives with greater ease. However, ineffective communication can lead to misunderstandings, conflicts, and missed opportunities.

One of the first steps in establishing effective communication channels is creating an environment that encourages open and honest communication. Team members should feel comfortable expressing their thoughts, opinions, and concerns without fear of judgment or repercussions. This can be achieved by promoting active listening, creating a non-judgmental space for discussions, and encouraging regular feedback from all team members.

Another important aspect of effective communication is choosing the right channels for different types of communication. While face-to-face meetings can be ideal for complex discussions and brainstorming sessions, email or project management tools may be more suitable for conveying quick updates or sharing documents. It is crucial to select the most appropriate communication method based on the nature and urgency of the information being shared.

Furthermore, establishing clear guidelines for communication is essential for ensuring consistent and efficient communication within the team. This includes setting expectations for response times, defining the appropriate use of communication tools, and establishing protocols for handling conflicts or disagreements. Regularly reviewing and revising these guidelines can help teams adapt to changing circumstances and improve their communication practices over time.

In conclusion, effective communication is a vital component of successful teamwork. By establishing clear and efficient communication channels, teams can enhance collaboration, productivity, and overall performance. It is important for team members to feel comfortable expressing their thoughts and concerns, and to choose the most appropriate communication method for each situation. By following the strategies outlined in this subchapter, any team can improve their communication practices and achieve greater success in their endeavors.

Chapter 3: Fostering a Positive Team Culture

Creating a Supportive and Inclusive Environment

In today's fast-paced and interconnected world, teamwork has become an essential skill in almost every setting. Whether you're working in a corporate office, a non-profit organization, or a small entrepreneurial venture, the ability to collaborate effectively with others is crucial for success. However, building a successful team requires more than just assembling a group of talented individuals. It requires creating a supportive and inclusive environment where everyone feels valued and can thrive.

In this subchapter of "Teamwork Triumph: Mastering Leadership in Every Setting," we will explore the key principles and strategies for creating a supportive and inclusive environment that promotes teamwork and unlocks the full potential of every team member. Regardless of your role or industry, these principles can be applied to cultivate a positive team culture and enhance collaboration.

First and foremost, fostering a supportive environment starts with effective communication. Encourage open and honest dialogue among team members, where opinions are respected, and ideas are welcomed. Actively listen to others and provide constructive feedback to promote continuous growth and learning. By creating a safe space for sharing thoughts, concerns, and suggestions, you foster a sense of belonging and trust within the team.

Secondly, inclusivity is vital for a successful team. Embrace diversity and recognize the unique strengths and perspectives each team member brings. Celebrate differences and create opportunities for everyone to contribute and shine. Foster a culture of inclusion by promoting equal opportunities and fair treatment for all team members, regardless of their background, gender, or ethnicity.

Another key aspect of a supportive and inclusive environment is providing adequate support and resources to team members. Ensure that everyone has the necessary tools, training, and support to excel in their roles. Encourage professional development and create a culture of continuous learning. By investing in the growth and well-being of your team, you demonstrate your commitment to their success and foster a sense of loyalty and dedication.

Lastly, lead by example. As a leader, your behavior sets the tone for the team. Demonstrate empathy, respect, and integrity in your actions and decisions. Encourage teamwork and collaboration by modeling these behaviors yourself. By being an inclusive and supportive leader, you inspire your team members to do the same.

In conclusion, creating a supportive and inclusive environment is essential for successful teamwork in any setting. By fostering open communication, embracing diversity, providing support and resources, and leading by example, you can cultivate a positive team culture where every individual feels valued and can thrive. Remember, teamwork triumphs when everyone feels included and supported.

Encouraging Collaboration and Cooperation

In today's fast-paced world, teamwork has become an essential component of success. Whether you are working in an office, participating in a sports team, or even involved in a community project, the ability to collaborate and cooperate with others is crucial. This subchapter will delve into the importance of fostering collaboration and cooperation within teams and provide practical strategies for achieving synergy and achieving remarkable results.

The foundation of effective teamwork lies in collaboration, where individuals come together to share their unique perspectives, skills, and knowledge. By encouraging collaboration, teams can harness the power of diversity and unlock innovative solutions that can propel them towards success. Collaboration also promotes a sense of belonging and unity, as team members feel valued and included in the decision-making process. This fosters a positive and supportive team culture, where everyone feels motivated to contribute their best.

Cooperation is another vital aspect of teamwork, as it involves individuals working together towards a common goal. Cooperation requires effective communication, active listening, and a willingness to compromise. It is crucial for team members to understand that their individual success is intertwined with the success of the team as a whole. By promoting cooperation, teams can overcome challenges more efficiently, capitalize on each other's strengths, and achieve outstanding results.

To encourage collaboration and cooperation within a team, leaders should create an environment that fosters trust and open communication. Team members should feel comfortable expressing their ideas, opinions, and concerns without fear of judgment or retribution. Regular team meetings and brainstorming sessions can provide a platform for collaboration, where everyone's input is valued and encouraged.

Additionally, team leaders can implement team-building activities and exercises to promote collaboration and cooperation. These activities can range from icebreaker games to problem-solving challenges, designed to foster trust, empathy, and effective communication among team members. By engaging in such activities, team members can build stronger relationships, understand each other's strengths and weaknesses, and develop a shared sense of purpose.

In conclusion, teamwork is a vital skill that transcends all areas of life. Encouraging collaboration and cooperation within a team is essential for achieving remarkable results. By fostering a culture of collaboration, teams can tap into the diverse perspectives and talents of its members. Likewise, by promoting cooperation, teams can work together towards a common goal, leveraging each other's strengths and overcoming challenges more effectively. With these strategies in place, teams can unlock their full potential and achieve triumph in any setting.

Celebrating Diversity and Individual Strengths

In today's interconnected and globalized world, celebrating diversity and recognizing individual strengths have become essential components of successful teamwork. In this subchapter, we will explore the importance of embracing our differences and leveraging our unique abilities to foster a harmonious and high-performing team.

Diversity encompasses various aspects, including but not limited to race, gender, age, nationality, and cultural background. When teams are composed of individuals from diverse backgrounds, they bring a rich tapestry of perspectives, experiences, and skills to the table. This diversity of thought and approach fuels creativity, innovation, and problem-solving, enabling teams to tackle complex challenges from multiple angles.

However, celebrating diversity goes beyond merely having a diverse team. It requires creating an inclusive environment where everyone feels valued, respected, and empowered to contribute their best. By fostering an atmosphere of inclusion, teams can unlock the full potential of each individual, allowing them to thrive and bring their unique strengths to the forefront.

Recognizing and appreciating individual strengths is an integral part of celebrating diversity. Each team member possesses a set of skills, talents, and experiences that make them unique. By understanding and leveraging these strengths, teams can effectively distribute tasks, allocate responsibilities, and maximize productivity. When individuals are assigned roles that align with their strengths, they are more likely to excel and contribute to the team's success.

Moreover, celebrating diversity and individual strengths also promotes a sense of belonging and camaraderie within the team. When team members feel valued for who they are and what they bring to the table, they are more likely to develop trust, build strong relationships, and collaborate seamlessly. This, in turn, leads to a positive team dynamic, increased motivation, and improved overall performance.

To create a culture that celebrates diversity and individual strengths, leaders must prioritize open communication, active listening, and empathy. They should encourage team members to share their perspectives, challenge assumptions, and learn from one another. Additionally, leaders should provide opportunities for personal and professional growth, allowing team members to build upon their strengths and develop new skills.

In conclusion, celebrating diversity and individual strengths is crucial for effective teamwork. By embracing our differences, fostering inclusion, and leveraging each person's unique abilities, teams can achieve remarkable success. Let us embrace diversity and unlock the full potential of our teams, creating a world where everyone's strengths are celebrated and valued.

Chapter 4: Effective Leadership Strategies

Leading by Example

In the realm of teamwork, effective leadership is crucial for success. It sets the tone, establishes the vision, and motivates team members to give their best. One key aspect of leadership that cannot be emphasized enough is leading by example. This subchapter delves into the significance of this leadership approach and illustrates how it can be harnessed to achieve triumph in any setting.

Leading by example is not just a catchy phrase; it is a powerful tool that can inspire and influence others. When leaders embody the qualities they expect from their team members, they create an environment of trust, respect, and accountability. By consistently demonstrating the behaviors and actions they desire from their team, leaders foster a culture of excellence and encourage others to do the same.

One of the fundamental aspects of leading by example is integrity. Leaders who act with honesty, transparency, and ethical behavior instill these values in their team. They become role models, guiding their members to do the right thing, even in challenging situations. When leaders uphold a high moral standard, it creates a sense of pride and unity within the team, resulting in increased productivity and better collaboration.

In addition to integrity, leaders must also exhibit passion and dedication. By showing enthusiasm for their work, leaders inspire their team members to believe in the mission and vision. When leaders consistently go above and beyond, it motivates others to do the same, leading to higher levels of achievement and success. Passionate leaders create an environment where everyone feels valued and encouraged to contribute their best efforts.

Leading by example also involves effective communication. Leaders who actively listen, provide clear instructions, and offer constructive feedback set the stage for open and honest dialogue within the team. When leaders communicate effectively, they foster a culture of collaboration, where ideas are shared, problems are solved collectively, and everyone feels comfortable expressing their opinions. This leads to enhanced creativity, innovation, and problem-solving capabilities.

In conclusion, leading by example is a leadership approach that is essential for achieving triumph in any setting, especially in the context of teamwork. By embodying the qualities they desire from their team members, leaders establish a culture of integrity, passion, dedication, and effective communication. This approach motivates team members to work together, fosters trust, and ultimately leads to success. Whether you are a leader or a team member, embracing the principle of leading by example can transform your team into a high-performing unit capable of conquering any challenge.

Setting Realistic Goals and Expectations

In the realm of teamwork, setting realistic goals and expectations is crucial for success. Whether you are working in a corporate setting, a sports team, or any other collaborative environment, understanding how to establish achievable objectives is key to fostering productivity and maintaining motivation among team members. In this subchapter, we will explore the importance of setting realistic goals and expectations and provide practical strategies to help you effectively navigate this process.

One of the main reasons why setting realistic goals is significant is that it allows individuals and teams to stay focused and motivated. When goals are too ambitious or unattainable, it can lead to frustration and demotivation. On the other hand, setting goals that are too easy can result in complacency and a lack of growth. By finding the right balance and setting goals that challenge but are still achievable, teams can maintain a healthy level of motivation and drive.

Another key aspect of setting realistic goals is ensuring effective communication and alignment among team members. It is essential to involve everyone in the goal-setting process to ensure that expectations are clear and understood by all. Encouraging open dialogue and actively listening to each team member's input will foster a sense of ownership and commitment, increasing the likelihood of achieving the set goals.

Furthermore, setting realistic goals helps in managing resources efficiently. When goals are well-defined and achievable, teams can allocate resources effectively, ensuring that time, energy, and expertise are utilized optimally. This approach minimizes the risk of burnout and prevents the team from spreading themselves too thin.

To establish realistic goals and expectations, it is vital to create a framework that takes into account various factors such as the team's capabilities, available resources, and the specific context in which they operate. By conducting a thorough analysis and considering these aspects, teams can set attainable objectives that align with their overall mission and vision.

In conclusion, setting realistic goals and expectations is a fundamental aspect of successful teamwork. By finding the right balance between challenging and achievable goals, involving all team members in the goal-setting process, and considering available resources, teams can foster motivation, effective communication, and optimal resource management. Ultimately, mastering the art of setting realistic goals and expectations will enable teams to achieve triumph in any collaborative setting.

Motivating and Inspiring Team Members

Motivating and inspiring team members is a fundamental aspect of effective teamwork. When team members are motivated, they are more likely to perform at their best, collaborate effectively, and achieve outstanding results. In this subchapter, we will delve into the key strategies and techniques that leaders can employ to boost motivation and inspire their team members to reach new heights of success.

One of the most powerful ways to motivate team members is by fostering a sense of purpose and meaning in their work. When team members understand how their individual contributions fit into the bigger picture and how their efforts contribute to the team's overall goals, they are more likely to feel a sense of fulfillment and motivation. Leaders can achieve this by clearly communicating the team's mission, vision, and objectives, and by highlighting the impact of each team member's role.

Recognition and appreciation also play a crucial role in motivating team members. People thrive when their efforts are acknowledged and valued. Leaders should regularly provide positive feedback, publicly recognize exceptional performance, and celebrate team milestones and achievements. This creates a positive environment that encourages team members to continue striving for excellence.

Another effective strategy is to empower team members by giving them autonomy and ownership over their work. When individuals feel trusted and empowered to make decisions, they are more likely to take ownership of their responsibilities and demonstrate initiative. Leaders can achieve this by delegating tasks and responsibilities, providing resources and support, and allowing team members to have a say in decision-making processes.

Furthermore, setting clear and challenging goals can inspire team members to push their limits and achieve remarkable results. Goals should be specific, measurable, attainable, relevant, and time-bound (SMART). Regularly revisiting and reassessing these goals helps team members stay focused and motivated.

Finally, leaders should lead by example and embody the qualities they want to see in their team members. A leader who demonstrates passion, resilience, and a positive attitude will inspire team members to adopt similar traits. By creating a positive and supportive team culture, leaders can foster a collaborative and motivating environment.

In conclusion, motivating and inspiring team members is essential for achieving success in any team setting. By creating a sense of purpose, recognizing achievements, empowering individuals, setting challenging goals, and leading by example, leaders can cultivate a highly motivated and inspired team. When team members feel motivated, they are more likely to collaborate effectively, perform at their best, and achieve outstanding results.

Chapter 5: Developing Essential Leadership Skills

Effective Communication Techniques

In any team setting, effective communication is the foundation for success. It is the key that unlocks the potential of teamwork, allowing individuals to collaborate, share ideas, and work towards a common goal. Whether you are a leader, a team member, or someone who aspires to be a part of a successful team, mastering effective communication techniques is crucial.

One of the most important aspects of effective communication is active listening. This means truly engaging with what others are saying, without interrupting or formulating a response before they have finished speaking. Active listening allows for better understanding, minimizes misunderstandings, and shows respect for the speaker. Additionally, it is important to ask clarifying questions to ensure that everyone is on the same page.

Another technique for effective communication is the use of non-verbal cues. Body language, facial expressions, and gestures can convey a wealth of information and help to reinforce the spoken message. Being aware of your own non-verbal cues and interpreting those of others can greatly enhance communication within a team.

Clear and concise language is also essential for effective communication. Avoid using jargon or technical terms that may not be understood by all team members. Instead, use simple and straightforward language to ensure that your message is easily understood by everyone. Additionally, it is important to be mindful of tone and delivery. A respectful and positive tone can go a long way in fostering open and honest communication within a team.

Furthermore, feedback plays a crucial role in effective communication within a team. Providing constructive feedback in a timely manner helps team members to grow and improve. It is important to focus on specific behaviors or actions rather than personal attacks, and to offer suggestions for improvement. Receiving feedback with an open mind and a willingness to learn is equally important for effective communication within a team.

In conclusion, effective communication techniques are vital for successful teamwork. Active listening, non-verbal cues, clear and concise language, and providing and receiving feedback are all essential components of effective communication. By mastering these techniques, individuals can contribute to a positive team dynamic, enhance collaboration, and achieve remarkable results. Whether you are a leader or a team member, understanding and practicing effective communication techniques will greatly benefit you in every team setting.

Active Listening and Feedback

In the fast-paced and interconnected world we live in today, effective teamwork has become more important than ever. Whether you are working in a corporate setting, a small business, a non-profit organization, or even a sports team, the ability to work well with others is a crucial skill that can make or break your success. One of the key components of successful teamwork is active listening and feedback.

Active listening is the act of fully engaging with what others are saying, not just hearing their words but truly understanding their meaning. It involves giving your full attention to the speaker, maintaining eye contact, and being present in the moment. By actively listening, you demonstrate respect for your teammates and create an environment that fosters open communication and collaboration.

Feedback plays a significant role in improving teamwork. It provides constructive criticism and helps individuals and teams grow and develop. When giving feedback, it is essential to be specific, objective, and focused on the behavior or task at hand. It is crucial to provide feedback promptly, in a non-judgmental manner, and with the intention of helping the person or team improve. Similarly, receiving feedback gracefully and with an open mind is equally important. When receiving feedback, try to view it as an opportunity for growth and learning rather than as a personal attack.

Active listening and feedback go hand in hand. By actively listening to your teammates, you are better able to understand their perspectives, needs, and concerns. This understanding allows you to provide meaningful and relevant feedback that can lead to positive changes in the team's dynamics and performance.

In the book "Teamwork Triumph: Mastering Leadership in Every Setting," we delve into the importance of active listening and feedback in enhancing teamwork. Through real-life examples, practical tips, and interactive exercises, this subchapter provides invaluable insights into becoming a better listener and a more effective giver and receiver of feedback.

Whether you are a team leader, a team member, or someone aspiring to improve their teamwork skills, this subchapter will equip you with the tools and techniques needed to create a collaborative and high-performing team environment. By mastering active listening and feedback, you will not only enhance your own leadership abilities but also contribute to the overall success of your team.

Remember, teamwork is not just about completing tasks; it is about building relationships, fostering trust, and achieving common goals. Active listening and feedback are the cornerstones of effective teamwork, and by incorporating these skills into your daily interactions, you will pave the way for triumph in any setting.

Conflict Resolution and Problem Solving

In any team setting, conflicts and problems are bound to arise. However, the true measure of a successful team lies in its ability to effectively resolve conflicts and find solutions to problems. This subchapter delves into the crucial aspects of conflict resolution and problem solving, providing valuable insights and practical strategies for mastering these skills in every team setting.

Conflict resolution is the process of addressing and resolving disagreements or disputes between team members. It is essential for maintaining a harmonious and productive team environment. The first step in conflict resolution is acknowledging the conflict and understanding its root causes. This requires active listening and open communication among team members. By encouraging everyone to express their viewpoints and concerns, teams can gain a deeper understanding of the conflict and work towards resolving it.

One effective approach to conflict resolution is the win-win strategy, where both parties involved in the conflict work together to find a mutually beneficial solution. This requires a willingness to compromise and collaborate. By focusing on common goals and shared interests, teams can often find creative solutions that satisfy everyone involved.

Problem solving, on the other hand, involves identifying and resolving issues or challenges that hinder team progress. It requires a systematic approach and the ability to analyze problems from different angles. The subchapter explores various problem-solving techniques, such as brainstorming, root cause analysis, and decision-making frameworks. These techniques help teams to generate innovative ideas, identify the underlying causes of problems, and make well-informed decisions.

Furthermore, effective problem solving in teams requires a supportive and non-judgmental atmosphere. Team members should feel comfortable sharing their thoughts and ideas without fear of criticism. By fostering a culture of trust and open communication, teams can enhance their problem-solving capabilities and tap into the collective wisdom of the group.

Ultimately, conflict resolution and problem solving are vital skills for successful teamwork. By mastering these skills, teams can overcome disagreements, navigate challenges, and achieve their goals with greater efficiency and harmony. This subchapter serves as a comprehensive guide, equipping individuals from all walks of life with the necessary tools to become effective conflict resolvers and problem solvers in any team setting.

Chapter 6: Empowering and Delegating

Trusting and Empowering Team Members

In the world of teamwork, trust and empowerment play a pivotal role in achieving success. When team members feel trusted and empowered, they are more likely to take ownership of their work, collaborate effectively, and contribute their best efforts towards the team's goals. This subchapter aims to explore the significance of trust and empowerment in building a strong and cohesive team, while providing valuable insights on how to cultivate these qualities within team members.

Trust is the foundation upon which successful teams are built. Without trust, communication breaks down, conflicts arise, and productivity suffers. Trusting team members creates an environment where open and honest communication can thrive. When team members trust each other, they feel comfortable sharing their ideas, concerns, and feedback, leading to improved problem-solving and innovation. Trust also fosters a sense of psychological safety, enabling individuals to take risks and learn from failures without fear of judgement. Leaders must lead by example, demonstrate trustworthiness, and encourage open dialogue to develop a culture of trust within their teams.

Empowering team members is equally important as it nurtures their confidence, motivation, and growth. By delegating tasks and responsibilities, leaders show their trust in their team members' abilities. Empowerment encourages individuals to take initiative, make decisions, and contribute their unique skills and perspectives.

This not only enhances their sense of ownership but also leads to increased job satisfaction and engagement. Leaders can empower their team members by providing them with autonomy, resources, and support to accomplish their goals. Regular feedback and recognition also play a crucial role in empowering team members, as it reinforces their sense of value and contribution to the team's overall success.

To cultivate trust and empowerment within a team, it is essential to foster a culture of transparency, respect, and collaboration. Open communication channels, regular team meetings, and team-building activities can help team members build rapport and develop trust. Leaders should also create opportunities for skill development and growth, providing team members with the tools and resources they need to excel in their roles. By setting clear expectations and establishing a supportive environment, leaders can empower their team members to take ownership of their work and make meaningful contributions.

In conclusion, trust and empowerment are the cornerstones of successful teamwork. By creating a culture of trust and empowering team members, leaders can foster collaboration, innovation, and productivity within their teams. Trusting and empowering team members not only enhances their individual growth and job satisfaction but also leads to overall team success.

Delegating Tasks and Responsibilities

In the world of teamwork, effective delegation is an essential skill that can lead to success and productivity. Delegating tasks and responsibilities not only lightens the load for leaders but also empowers team members to take ownership and contribute their unique skills and expertise. This subchapter explores the art of delegation and provides practical strategies for mastering this crucial aspect of leadership in every setting.

1. The Importance of Delegation
Delegation is not about passing off work but rather about making the most efficient use of resources. By assigning tasks and responsibilities to team members who are best suited for them, leaders can free up their own time and focus on higher-level strategic activities. Furthermore, delegation fosters professional growth and development among team members, enabling them to enhance their skills and take on more challenging roles.

2. Assessing the Right Fit
Before delegating tasks, leaders must assess each team member's strengths, weaknesses, and interests. By matching tasks to individuals who possess the necessary skill set, leaders can ensure that the work is completed effectively and efficiently. Additionally, it is important to consider the developmental needs of team members, offering them opportunities to stretch their abilities and learn new skills.

3. Clear Communication
Effective delegation hinges on clear and concise communication. Leaders should clearly articulate the task's objectives, expectations, and any relevant guidelines or deadlines. It is vital to provide team

members with all the information and resources they need to successfully complete the task. Regular check-ins and open lines of communication are key to ensuring that everyone is on the same page and any potential issues are addressed promptly.

4. Building Trust

Delegation requires trust between leaders and team members. Leaders must have confidence in their team's abilities and allow them to make decisions and take ownership of their work. By demonstrating trust, leaders promote a sense of autonomy and responsibility among team members, fostering a positive and empowering work environment.

5. Recognizing and Rewarding Success

As team members successfully complete delegated tasks and responsibilities, it is essential to acknowledge their efforts and celebrate their achievements. Recognizing and rewarding success not only boosts morale but also reinforces the importance of delegation and encourages future engagement and commitment.

In conclusion, delegation is a fundamental aspect of effective teamwork and leadership. By delegating tasks and responsibilities, leaders can optimize productivity, foster professional growth, and build trust within their teams. Clear communication, assessing the right fit, and recognizing success are crucial elements in mastering delegation in every setting. By embracing the power of delegation, leaders can unlock the full potential of their teams and achieve triumph in any collaborative endeavor.

Providing Support and Resources

In the fast-paced world we live in, teamwork has become an essential component of success in almost every setting. Whether you are part of a corporate team, a sports team, or any other group working towards a common goal, effective teamwork is crucial. However, achieving true collaboration and synergy within a team is not always an easy task. It requires effort, dedication, and most importantly, providing support and resources to team members.

Supporting your team members is not just about being there for them when they need a helping hand. It goes beyond that. It means creating an environment where everyone feels valued, heard, and empowered. One way to provide support is by fostering open communication channels. Encourage team members to express their ideas, concerns, and feedback freely. Actively listen to them, show empathy, and provide constructive feedback. This will not only improve the overall team dynamics but also enhance individual growth and development.

Another crucial aspect of support is recognizing and appreciating the efforts of your team members. Celebrate their successes, acknowledge their hard work, and motivate them to keep pushing forward. Remember, a simple word of appreciation can go a long way in boosting morale and encouraging team members to give their best.

Resources play a significant role in enabling teams to achieve their goals. As a leader, it is your responsibility to ensure that your team has the necessary tools, equipment, and information required for their tasks. This could involve providing training programs, investing in technology, or securing funding. By providing the right resources, you empower your team members to perform at their best and overcome any obstacles that may come their way.

Furthermore, support and resources are not limited to just the leader of a team. Each team member has a role to play in providing support to their colleagues. Collaboration and cooperation are key. Encourage team members to share their knowledge and expertise with each other. Foster a culture of mutual assistance and create opportunities for cross-training and skill development.

In conclusion, providing support and resources is essential for effective teamwork. By creating a supportive environment, recognizing and appreciating efforts, and ensuring the availability of necessary resources, teams can thrive and achieve remarkable results. Remember, teamwork triumphs when every individual feels supported and empowered to contribute their best.

Chapter 7: Leading Through Change and Challenges

Adapting to Change and Embracing Innovation

In today's fast-paced and ever-evolving world, the ability to adapt to change and embrace innovation is crucial for success in any field. This is especially true in the realm of teamwork, where collaboration and cooperation are essential for achieving common goals. In this subchapter, we will explore the importance of adapting to change and the benefits of embracing innovation in order to master leadership in any setting.

Change is an inevitable part of life, and it often presents challenges and opportunities. Those who are resistant to change may find themselves left behind, while those who embrace it can thrive and excel. Adapting to change requires a flexible mindset and a willingness to let go of old ways of doing things. This can be particularly challenging in a team setting, where different individuals may have different comfort levels with change. However, by fostering a culture of openness and continuous learning, teams can create an environment that encourages the adaptation to change.

Embracing innovation is closely tied to adapting to change. Innovation is about finding new ways of doing things, challenging the status quo, and thinking outside the box. It requires a mindset that is open to experimentation and risk-taking. By encouraging team members to embrace innovation, leaders can foster a culture of creativity and problem-solving. This can lead to breakthroughs and advancements that propel the team towards success.

There are numerous benefits to adapting to change and embracing innovation in a team setting. Firstly, it allows teams to stay relevant and competitive in a rapidly changing world. By constantly adapting and innovating, teams can keep up with emerging trends and technologies, ensuring that their work remains cutting-edge and impactful.

Additionally, adapting to change and embracing innovation can lead to increased motivation and engagement among team members. When individuals feel that their ideas and input are valued, they are more likely to be invested in the team's goals and objectives. This can result in higher levels of productivity and collaboration.

In conclusion, adapting to change and embracing innovation are essential skills for mastering leadership in any setting, particularly in the context of teamwork. By cultivating a mindset that is open to change and encouraging team members to embrace innovation, leaders can create a dynamic and thriving team culture. This, in turn, leads to increased adaptability, creativity, and productivity, ultimately driving the team towards success.

Managing Conflict and Overcoming Obstacles

In any team setting, conflict and obstacles are bound to arise. It is essential to understand that conflict is not necessarily a negative aspect of teamwork; in fact, it can be an opportunity for growth and innovation. By proactively managing conflict and overcoming obstacles, teams can foster a more harmonious and productive work environment.

One of the key steps in managing conflict is open communication. Encouraging team members to express their thoughts and concerns freely can help prevent misunderstandings and potential conflicts. Active listening is equally important; it allows team members to understand different perspectives and find common ground. By promoting open and honest dialogue, teams can resolve conflicts efficiently and effectively.

Another crucial aspect of managing conflict is addressing it early on. Ignoring or avoiding conflicts only allows them to fester and escalate, potentially causing irreparable damage to relationships and team dynamics. Instead, team leaders should proactively identify and address conflicts as soon as they arise, encouraging all parties involved to find mutually beneficial solutions.

In addition to conflict, teams often encounter various obstacles that can hinder progress and success. These obstacles may include resource constraints, time limitations, resistance to change, or lack of clarity in goals and roles. To overcome these obstacles, it is essential for teams to adopt a problem-solving mindset.

Firstly, teams should assess the situation and identify the root causes of the obstacles. This requires a deep understanding of the team's objectives, as well as the ability to analyze and prioritize the challenges at hand. Once the obstacles are identified, teams can brainstorm potential solutions and evaluate their feasibility and impact. Collaboration and creativity are key during this stage, as different perspectives can lead to innovative problem-solving approaches.

Furthermore, teams should be adaptable and flexible in their approach to overcoming obstacles. Sometimes, unforeseen circumstances may require teams to adjust their strategies and plans. By maintaining open lines of communication and a willingness to adapt, teams can navigate obstacles with resilience and agility.

Lastly, celebrating small victories along the way can boost team morale and motivation. Recognizing and appreciating the efforts made to overcome obstacles encourages team members to continue working together towards shared goals.

In conclusion, managing conflict and overcoming obstacles are integral to successful teamwork. By fostering open communication, addressing conflicts promptly, adopting a problem-solving mindset, and staying adaptable, teams can navigate challenges and achieve triumphs. Embracing conflict as an opportunity for growth and viewing obstacles as stepping stones towards success, teams can create a harmonious and collaborative work environment that empowers every individual to contribute their best.

Learning from Failures and Turning Them into Opportunities

We all face failures at some point in our lives, whether it's in our personal relationships, academic pursuits, or professional careers. However, what sets successful individuals apart is their ability to learn from these failures and turn them into opportunities for growth and success. In this subchapter, we will explore the importance of learning from failures and how to effectively do so within the context of teamwork.

Failure is not something to be feared or avoided; rather, it is a stepping stone towards success. When we fail, it provides us with valuable insights into our weaknesses and areas for improvement. It allows us to reflect on our actions and decisions, helping us identify what went wrong and why. By analyzing our failures, we gain a deeper understanding of ourselves and our team dynamics, enabling us to make better choices in the future.

One of the key aspects of learning from failures is maintaining a growth mindset. Instead of viewing failures as setbacks or personal flaws, we should see them as opportunities for learning and development. Embracing a growth mindset allows us to approach failures with resilience and determination, enabling us to bounce back stronger than before. It is through this process that we can uncover hidden potentials and discover innovative solutions to challenges.

In a team setting, learning from failures becomes even more crucial. When a team experiences failure, it is essential to foster an environment of psychological safety and open communication. Team members should feel comfortable sharing their failures and discussing the lessons learned without fear of judgment or retribution. Encouraging a culture of learning from failures not only strengthens the team's problem-solving capabilities but also promotes trust and collaboration.

To effectively learn from failures, it is important to adopt a systematic approach. This involves conducting post-mortem analyses, where the team reflects on the failure, identifies the root causes, and develops action plans to prevent similar mistakes in the future. Additionally, seeking feedback from team members, mentors, or experts can provide valuable insights and alternative perspectives on the failure.

Ultimately, by embracing failures as opportunities for growth and learning, we can transform setbacks into stepping stones towards success. Learning from failures strengthens our teamwork skills, enhances our problem-solving capabilities, and enables us to adapt and thrive in any setting. So, let us embrace failures, learn from them, and create a culture of continuous improvement and success in our teams and beyond.

Chapter 8: Inspiring and Motivating Teams

Recognizing and Appreciating Team Achievements

In the fast-paced and competitive world we live in, teamwork has become an essential component of success in every setting. Whether it is in the corporate world, sports arena, or even within families and communities, the ability to work together towards a common goal is crucial. However, simply working together is not enough; recognizing and appreciating team achievements is equally important.

When teams come together and accomplish great things, it is essential to acknowledge and celebrate their achievements. Recognizing team accomplishments not only boosts morale but also fosters a sense of camaraderie and motivates individuals to continue working hard towards future goals. It creates a positive work environment, fuels team spirit, and encourages collaboration.

One of the most effective ways to recognize and appreciate team achievements is through regular and timely feedback. When team members receive feedback on their efforts, they feel valued and acknowledged for their contributions. This can be done through both informal and formal methods, such as team meetings, one-on-one conversations, or even written notes of appreciation. By providing constructive feedback and highlighting specific achievements, team members are encouraged to continue their excellent work and strive for even greater success.

In addition to feedback, rewards and recognition programs can also play a significant role in appreciating team achievements. These programs can include incentives such as bonuses, promotions, or even team outings to celebrate milestones. By providing tangible rewards, team members feel a sense of accomplishment and are motivated to continue working towards their goals. It is important to tailor these rewards to the individual preferences and needs of the team, ensuring they are meaningful and impactful.

Another powerful way to recognize and appreciate team achievements is through public recognition. This can be done through company-wide announcements, newsletters, or even social media platforms. By publicly acknowledging team accomplishments, not only are team members recognized for their hard work, but it also showcases the organization's commitment to teamwork and encourages other teams to strive for success.

In conclusion, recognizing and appreciating team achievements is an essential aspect of mastering leadership in every setting. By providing timely feedback, implementing rewards and recognition programs, and publicly acknowledging team accomplishments, leaders can create a positive work environment that fosters team spirit, motivates individuals, and drives future success. Remember, a successful team is built on a foundation of appreciation and recognition.

Implementing Effective Rewards and Incentives

In any team setting, it is crucial to implement effective rewards and incentives to motivate and engage team members. Rewards and incentives play a key role in boosting team morale, fostering a positive work environment, and driving productivity. This subchapter aims to provide valuable insights on how to effectively implement rewards and incentives to maximize teamwork and achieve outstanding results.

Firstly, it is important to understand that rewards and incentives are not one-size-fits-all. Different individuals have different motivations, so it is essential to create a diverse range of rewards and incentives to cater to various preferences. Monetary rewards, such as bonuses or raises, can be effective for some team members, while others may be more motivated by recognition, career development opportunities, or non-monetary perks like extra vacation days or flexible work hours. By offering a variety of rewards, leaders can ensure that each team member feels valued and acknowledged.

Furthermore, it is vital to link rewards and incentives directly to team goals and individual contributions. When team members can clearly see the connection between their efforts, achievements, and the rewards they receive, it reinforces their sense of purpose and increases their motivation to excel. This can be achieved by setting specific performance metrics and milestones, and transparently communicating the criteria for earning rewards. Regularly reviewing and updating these criteria ensures fairness and keeps team members motivated to continuously improve.

In addition to tangible rewards, creating a culture of appreciation is equally important. Simple gestures such as praising team members publicly for their accomplishments or expressing gratitude for their hard work can go a long way. Regularly acknowledging and celebrating achievements not only boosts team morale but also fosters a sense of camaraderie and unity among team members.

Lastly, it is crucial to regularly evaluate and reassess the effectiveness of the rewards and incentives implemented. Soliciting feedback from team members about their preferences and what motivates them can provide valuable insights for refining the rewards program. Additionally, staying updated on industry trends and best practices can help leaders stay ahead and continuously improve their approach.

In conclusion, implementing effective rewards and incentives is essential for promoting teamwork and achieving success in any setting. By tailoring rewards to individual preferences, linking them to team goals, fostering a culture of appreciation, and regularly evaluating their effectiveness, leaders can create a motivating and engaging environment that drives productivity and cultivates a high-performing team.

Creating a Culture of Continuous Learning and Growth

In the fast-paced and ever-evolving world of team work, it is imperative to foster a culture of continuous learning and growth. This subchapter aims to provide valuable insights and practical strategies on how to cultivate such a culture, equipping individuals and teams with the necessary tools to thrive in any setting.

To truly embrace the concept of continuous learning and growth, it is essential to promote a growth mindset. This mindset encourages individuals to view challenges as opportunities for growth rather than setbacks. By instilling a belief in the potential for improvement and development, teams can overcome obstacles with resilience and determination.

One of the key elements in creating a culture of continuous learning is the establishment of a safe and supportive environment. When team members feel comfortable sharing ideas, asking questions, and seeking feedback, they are more likely to take risks and embrace new learning experiences. Encouraging open and honest communication allows for the exchange of knowledge and promotes a sense of collective growth.

Another vital aspect of fostering continuous learning is providing access to resources and opportunities for development. This can include offering workshops, training sessions, and mentorship programs. By investing in the growth of team members, organizations demonstrate their commitment to their employees' professional growth and overall success.

Furthermore, incorporating learning and growth into the team's regular activities is essential. Encouraging regular reflection and debriefing sessions after completing projects or tasks enables individuals and teams to identify areas for improvement and implement changes accordingly. By creating a space for continuous feedback and reflection, teams can constantly evolve and enhance their performance.

Finally, leaders play a crucial role in cultivating a culture of continuous learning and growth. Leading by example, they should actively seek out opportunities for personal development and demonstrate a commitment to lifelong learning. Leaders who encourage, support, and reward continuous learning initiatives inspire their teams to do the same.

In conclusion, creating a culture of continuous learning and growth is imperative for success in teamwork. By promoting a growth mindset, fostering a safe and supportive environment, providing resources and opportunities for development, incorporating learning into regular activities, and leading by example, teams can embrace a culture of continuous improvement. With this mindset, individuals and teams can adapt to challenges, unlock their full potential, and achieve triumph in any setting.

Chapter 9: Leading Cross-Functional and Virtual Teams

Strategies for Leading Cross-Functional Teams

In today's fast-paced and interconnected world, cross-functional teams have become increasingly common in various industries. These teams consist of individuals with diverse skills, expertise, and backgrounds who come together to collaborate on a specific project or goal. Leading such teams requires a unique set of strategies to ensure success and maximize their potential.

1. Build a Strong Foundation: The first step in leading a cross-functional team is to establish a strong foundation. This involves clearly defining the team's purpose, objectives, and roles. It is essential to ensure that everyone understands their responsibilities and how their contributions align with the overall team goals.

2. Foster Communication and Collaboration: Effective communication and collaboration are vital for the success of cross-functional teams. Encourage open and honest communication among team members, ensuring that all opinions and perspectives are valued. Use collaborative tools and technologies to facilitate information sharing and teamwork, regardless of physical location.

3. Develop Trust and Respect: Trust and respect are crucial elements in any team setting, but they are particularly important in cross-functional teams due to the diverse backgrounds and expertise involved. As a leader, focus on building trust among team members by promoting transparency, active listening, and valuing each

person's contributions. Encourage a culture of respect where differences are seen as strengths rather than obstacles.

4. Set Clear Expectations: Clearly define expectations regarding deliverables, timelines, and quality standards. Ensure that each team member understands their individual and collective responsibilities. Regularly communicate progress and provide feedback to keep everyone aligned and motivated.

5. Manage Conflict Effectively: Cross-functional teams often face conflicts arising from different perspectives and goals. It is essential to address conflicts promptly and openly, encouraging constructive dialogue and finding win-win solutions. Use conflict resolution techniques, such as mediation or compromise, to maintain a harmonious working environment.

6. Empower and Delegate: Empowering team members to make decisions and take ownership of their work is critical for their engagement and productivity. Delegate tasks based on individual strengths and expertise, while providing necessary support and resources.

7. Encourage Continuous Learning: Foster a culture of continuous learning and improvement within the team. Encourage team members to share knowledge, skills, and best practices. Provide opportunities for professional development and training to enhance individual and team capabilities.

Leading cross-functional teams can be challenging, but with the right strategies, it can be a rewarding experience. By building a strong foundation, fostering communication and collaboration, developing trust and respect, setting clear expectations, managing conflicts effectively, empowering and delegating, and encouraging continuous learning, leaders can unlock the full potential of their cross-functional teams and achieve remarkable results.

Teamwork Triumph: Mastering Leadership in Every Setting offers comprehensive guidance on leading cross-functional teams and other aspects of teamwork. Whether you are a team leader, team member, or aspiring to be a leader, this book provides invaluable insights and practical strategies to enhance your effectiveness and success in any team setting.

Overcoming Challenges in Virtual Team Environments

In today's interconnected world, virtual teams have become increasingly prevalent, enabling teams to work together seamlessly regardless of geographical boundaries. However, along with the numerous benefits virtual teams offer, they also present unique challenges that need to be addressed in order to achieve successful teamwork.

One major challenge in virtual team environments is communication. Unlike traditional face-to-face teams, virtual teams rely heavily on technology to communicate. This reliance on technology can lead to misinterpretation, misunderstandings, and a lack of clarity. To overcome this challenge, it is essential to establish clear communication channels, set expectations for response times, and encourage frequent and open communication among team members. Utilizing video conferencing tools, instant messaging platforms, and project management software can also enhance communication and foster collaboration within virtual teams.

Another challenge that virtual teams face is building trust among team members. Trust is the foundation of any successful team, and without the ability to physically interact and observe one another, establishing trust in a virtual team can be more difficult. To overcome this challenge, team leaders should encourage team members to get to know each other personally, foster a sense of camaraderie, and create opportunities for team building activities. Regular virtual meetings, where team members can share their achievements, challenges, and progress, can also help build trust and create a sense of accountability.

Virtual team environments also require effective time management and organization skills. With team members working in different time zones, juggling different priorities, and facing potential distractions at home, it can be challenging to ensure everyone is aligned and working towards the same goals. To overcome this challenge, it is crucial to establish clear deadlines, set priorities, and establish a transparent workflow. Regular check-ins, progress updates, and utilizing project management tools can also help keep virtual teams on track and ensure everyone is working towards the same objectives.

In conclusion, virtual teams offer numerous advantages but also present unique challenges that need to be overcome for successful teamwork. By addressing communication issues, building trust among team members, and implementing effective time management strategies, virtual teams can triumph over these challenges and achieve exceptional results. Embracing the opportunities that virtual team environments provide and mastering the skills necessary for virtual teamwork will undoubtedly enhance collaboration and drive success in any setting.

Leveraging Technology for Effective Communication and Collaboration

In today's fast-paced and interconnected world, effective communication and collaboration have become essential skills for success in any team setting. With the advent of technology, we now have a wide range of tools and platforms that can greatly enhance our ability to work together seamlessly and efficiently. This subchapter will explore the various ways in which technology can be leveraged to improve teamwork and foster effective communication and collaboration.

One of the most significant benefits of technology in teamwork is the ability to communicate and collaborate in real-time, regardless of geographical barriers. With tools like video conferencing, instant messaging, and project management software, team members can easily connect and exchange ideas, regardless of their physical location. This allows for better coordination, quicker decision-making, and increased overall productivity.

Additionally, technology enables teams to share and access information easily. Cloud storage and file-sharing platforms provide a centralized location where team members can access and collaborate on documents, presentations, and other important files. This not only eliminates the need for constant email exchanges but also ensures that everyone is working on the most up-to-date version of a document, reducing confusion and improving efficiency.

Moreover, technology offers a wide array of collaboration tools that promote creativity and innovation within teams. Virtual whiteboards, brainstorming platforms, and project management software allow team members to contribute their ideas, track progress, and stay organized. These tools encourage active participation and ensure that everyone's voice is heard, fostering a sense of inclusivity and engagement.

However, it is important to note that while technology can greatly enhance teamwork, it is not a substitute for effective interpersonal skills. Face-to-face communication and building strong relationships are still crucial elements of successful teamwork. Technology should be used as a supplement to these traditional methods, rather than a replacement.

In conclusion, leveraging technology for effective communication and collaboration is vital in today's team-oriented work environments. By utilizing the various tools and platforms available, teams can overcome geographical barriers, share information efficiently, and foster creativity and innovation. However, it is essential to strike a balance between technology and interpersonal skills, recognizing that technology should enhance, but not replace, face-to-face communication and relationship-building. By embracing technology and utilizing it effectively, teams can experience heightened productivity, improved decision-making, and ultimately, triumph in their teamwork endeavors.

Chapter 10: Sustaining High-Performing Teams

Building Trust and Cohesion

In any setting, be it a professional organization, sports team, or community group, building trust and cohesion among team members is crucial for success. Trust is the foundation upon which effective teamwork is built, and without it, team dynamics can suffer, leading to decreased productivity and morale. This subchapter aims to explore the importance of trust and cohesion in teamwork and provide practical strategies for fostering these essential elements.

Trust is the glue that holds a team together. It is the belief that each team member will act in the best interest of the group, communicate honestly, and fulfill their responsibilities. Trust allows individuals to feel safe and supported, creating an environment where ideas can be freely shared, conflicts can be resolved constructively, and risks can be taken without fear of judgment or retribution.

To cultivate trust within a team, open and transparent communication is paramount. Encourage team members to express their thoughts, concerns, and ideas openly, while also actively listening to one another. This fosters a sense of psychological safety, where individuals feel comfortable being vulnerable and taking risks. Regular team meetings and check-ins can provide opportunities for everyone to contribute and stay updated on the team's progress.

Another crucial aspect of building trust is leading by example. As a leader or team member, demonstrate integrity, reliability, and accountability in your actions. Be consistent and follow through on commitments, as this builds credibility and reinforces trust among team members. Encourage trust-building exercises, such as team-building activities or trust falls, to enhance interpersonal connections and develop a shared sense of reliance.

Cohesion, on the other hand, refers to the unity and harmony within a team. When team members feel a strong bond and shared purpose, they are more likely to work collaboratively and support one another. To foster cohesion, create a team identity and establish clear goals and expectations. Encourage team members to celebrate achievements together and provide recognition for individual contributions.

Effective teamwork also requires a culture of inclusivity and respect. Embrace diversity within the team, valuing different perspectives and ideas. Encourage collaboration and cooperation, rather than competition, as this promotes a sense of collective achievement and shared success.

In conclusion, building trust and cohesion within a team is essential for maximizing productivity and creating a positive work environment. By prioritizing open communication, leading by example, and fostering a sense of unity, teams can overcome challenges and achieve extraordinary results. Remember, trust is the foundation, and cohesion is the catalyst that propels teamwork to triumph in every setting.

Promoting Work-Life Balance and Well-being

In today's fast-paced and demanding world, achieving a healthy work-life balance has become increasingly challenging for individuals across various professions. However, recognizing the importance of maintaining this balance is crucial to our overall well-being and success, especially in the context of teamwork.

Work-life balance refers to the equilibrium between our personal and professional lives. It involves allocating time and energy to various aspects of our lives, such as family, friends, hobbies, and self-care, in addition to our work commitments. This balance is essential not only for our mental and physical health but also for fostering effective teamwork and maximizing productivity.

When individuals are overwhelmed and exhausted due to an imbalanced lifestyle, it directly impacts their ability to contribute effectively within a team setting. Stress and burnout can lead to decreased motivation, diminished creativity, and strained relationships with colleagues. Therefore, promoting work-life balance within a team is crucial to ensure the overall success and well-being of its members.

There are several strategies that can be employed to promote work-life balance and well-being within a team. Firstly, organizations and team leaders must actively encourage open communication surrounding workloads and personal commitments. This creates a supportive environment where team members feel comfortable discussing their needs and concerns.

Furthermore, implementing flexible work arrangements, such as remote work options or flexible hours, can greatly contribute to work-life balance. This allows individuals to manage personal responsibilities and maintain a healthier lifestyle, ultimately enhancing their overall well-being and satisfaction.

Moreover, promoting the importance of self-care and setting boundaries is essential. Encouraging team members to prioritize their physical and mental health through exercise, adequate sleep, and relaxation techniques can significantly improve their ability to handle work-related challenges.

Lastly, fostering a culture of trust and respect within the team is paramount. When team members feel valued and supported, they are more likely to communicate openly and seek assistance when needed. This fosters a collaborative environment where workload distribution can be managed effectively, preventing individuals from becoming overwhelmed.

In conclusion, promoting work-life balance and well-being within a team is vital for maintaining a healthy and productive workforce. By implementing strategies such as open communication, flexible work arrangements, and emphasizing self-care, teams can create an environment where individuals thrive both personally and professionally. Ultimately, achieving work-life balance not only benefits team members individually but also elevates the overall success and harmony within the team.

Nurturing a Culture of Continuous Improvement

In today's fast-paced and ever-evolving world, the concept of continuous improvement has become crucial for individuals and organizations alike. It holds the key to unlocking success and achieving greatness in any team setting. Whether you are a leader, a member of a team, or someone interested in personal growth, nurturing a culture of continuous improvement is essential for achieving long-term success.

The power of teamwork lies not only in the collective efforts of its members but also in their ability to adapt, learn, and grow together. A culture of continuous improvement enables teams to constantly assess their performance, identify areas of improvement, and take proactive measures to enhance their skills and capabilities. It is a mindset that encourages innovation, collaboration, and an unwavering commitment to excellence.

One of the first steps in nurturing a culture of continuous improvement is to create an environment that encourages open communication and feedback. Team members should feel comfortable sharing their ideas, concerns, and suggestions without fear of judgment. This fosters a sense of trust and psychological safety, allowing for constructive criticism and the opportunity for growth.

To truly embrace continuous improvement, teams must also adopt a mindset of learning. This involves encouraging a thirst for knowledge, providing opportunities for training and development, and promoting a growth mindset among team members. By embracing a culture of learning, teams can stay ahead of the curve, adapt to new challenges, and continuously improve their performance.

Moreover, leaders play a crucial role in nurturing a culture of continuous improvement. They must lead by example, demonstrating a commitment to personal growth and development. Leaders should also encourage their team members to set goals, celebrate milestones, and provide ongoing support and resources to help them achieve their objectives.

In conclusion, nurturing a culture of continuous improvement is imperative for success in any team setting. It requires open communication, a mindset of learning, and strong leadership. By fostering an environment that encourages feedback, embraces learning, and supports personal growth, teams can continuously adapt, innovate, and improve their performance. Remember, the journey towards excellence is not a destination but a continuous process of growth and improvement.

Chapter 11: Leadership Beyond the Team

Influencing and Inspiring Others Outside the Team

In the world of teamwork, leaders are often faced with the challenge of influencing and inspiring individuals outside of their immediate team. Whether it's stakeholders, clients, or colleagues from different departments, effective leadership extends beyond the boundaries of a single team. In this subchapter, we explore the strategies and techniques that can help you become a master of influencing and inspiring others outside your team, ultimately leading to success in every setting.

One of the most important aspects of influencing and inspiring others is building strong relationships. Take the time to understand the needs, goals, and motivations of the individuals you are trying to influence. This will allow you to tailor your approach and communication style to resonate with them. Remember, it's not just about what you want; it's about finding common ground and aligning your objectives with theirs.

Another key element is effective communication. Be clear, concise, and persuasive in your messaging. Present your ideas in a compelling manner that captures the attention and interest of your audience. Use storytelling and real-life examples to illustrate your points and make them relatable. Additionally, active listening is crucial. Show genuine interest in what others have to say, ask questions, and seek feedback. This will not only make them feel valued but also provide you with valuable insights to further refine your approach.

Furthermore, leverage your expertise and credibility to establish yourself as a trusted authority. Demonstrate your knowledge and competence through your actions and achievements. Share your successes and lessons learned to inspire others and gain their trust. Be a resource and offer your support whenever needed. By doing so, you will position yourself as a valuable asset and someone worth listening to.

Finally, be adaptable and open-minded. Different individuals have different perspectives and approaches. Embrace diversity and seek to understand and appreciate different ways of thinking. Be willing to adjust your strategies and consider alternative viewpoints. This flexibility will not only make you more effective at influencing others but also foster a culture of collaboration and innovation within your team.

In conclusion, influencing and inspiring others outside the team is an essential skill for successful leadership in any setting. By building relationships, communicating effectively, establishing credibility, and remaining adaptable, you can become a master at influencing and inspiring individuals beyond your immediate team. Embrace these strategies, and watch as you create a ripple effect of positive change and collaboration throughout your organization.

Collaborating with Other Leaders for Organizational Success

In today's fast-paced and interconnected world, teamwork has become increasingly important for organizational success. No longer can leaders rely solely on their own expertise and skills to drive their organizations forward. Instead, they must learn to collaborate effectively with other leaders to achieve common goals and propel their teams to new heights. This subchapter explores the power of collaboration and how it can enhance teamwork and overall organizational success.

Leadership is not about working in isolation; it is about effectively working with others to bring out the best in everyone. By collaborating with other leaders, you can tap into a wealth of diverse perspectives, experiences, and knowledge. This rich pool of resources can help you make better decisions, solve complex problems, and create innovative solutions that may not have been possible otherwise. When leaders come together, they can leverage their collective strengths to drive organizational success.

Successful collaboration requires open communication, trust, and a shared vision. Leaders must be willing to listen to each other, respect different viewpoints, and build strong relationships based on trust and mutual respect. By fostering a collaborative culture, leaders can create an environment where teamwork thrives and everyone feels valued and included.

Collaboration between leaders also extends beyond the boundaries of their own teams. It involves partnering with leaders from different departments, divisions, or even organizations to achieve shared objectives. This cross-functional collaboration allows leaders to leverage diverse expertise and resources, break down silos, and promote a holistic approach to problem-solving. It encourages a sense of unity and shared responsibility, ultimately leading to improved performance and organizational success.

To enhance collaboration with other leaders, it is essential to foster a culture of teamwork throughout the organization. This can be achieved by promoting open communication channels, encouraging knowledge sharing, and recognizing and celebrating collaborative achievements. Leaders should also provide opportunities for cross-functional collaboration, such as team-building activities, workshops, or joint projects, to strengthen relationships and promote a collaborative mindset.

In conclusion, collaborating with other leaders is a fundamental aspect of effective leadership and organizational success. By harnessing the power of collaboration, leaders can tap into a diverse range of perspectives and resources, solve complex problems, and drive innovation. Moreover, collaboration fosters a sense of unity and shared responsibility, promoting a culture of teamwork that enhances overall organizational performance. Embrace collaboration, and you will propel your team and organization to triumph in every setting.

Leaving a Legacy: Developing Future Leaders

In our quest to achieve success, it is crucial that we not only focus on our individual accomplishments, but also on the legacy we leave behind. As leaders, it is our responsibility to develop and nurture the next generation of leaders who will continue to foster the spirit of teamwork and collaboration in every setting.

Teamwork is the cornerstone of success in any field or industry. It brings diverse perspectives together, encourages innovation, and fosters a sense of belonging and shared purpose. However, without effective leadership, even the most talented teams can struggle to reach their full potential. That is why it is essential for us to prioritize the development of future leaders who can continue to build upon the foundations we have laid.

Developing future leaders involves more than just providing them with technical skills or knowledge. It requires instilling in them the values and principles that underpin successful teamwork. These values include integrity, empathy, effective communication, and the ability to inspire and motivate others. By nurturing these qualities in the next generation, we ensure that the legacy of teamwork continues to thrive.

One of the most powerful ways to develop future leaders is through mentorship. By serving as mentors, we can share our wisdom, experiences, and insights with aspiring leaders. This not only helps them develop their skills and knowledge but also instills in them the importance of teamwork and collaboration. As mentors, we have the opportunity to guide them through challenges, provide feedback, and encourage their growth.

Another valuable tool for developing future leaders is providing opportunities for them to lead and take ownership of projects or initiatives. By empowering them to make decisions and assume responsibility, we allow them to develop their leadership skills and gain confidence in their abilities. This hands-on experience not only enhances their understanding of teamwork but also helps them develop their unique leadership style.

As we work towards leaving a legacy of effective teamwork and leadership, it is important to remember that developing future leaders is an ongoing process. It requires continuous investment and commitment. By actively seeking out opportunities to mentor, empower, and inspire others, we ensure that the spirit of teamwork continues to flourish and propel organizations and communities forward.

In conclusion, leaving a legacy of developing future leaders is a vital aspect of mastering leadership in every setting. By prioritizing the development of the next generation of leaders, we ensure that the values and principles of effective teamwork and collaboration are carried forward. Through mentorship, empowerment, and continuous investment, we can shape a future where teamwork triumphs, and leadership thrives.

Chapter 12: Conclusion: Mastering Leadership in Every Setting

Reflecting on the Journey

In the realm of teamwork, success is not just about reaching the destination; it is about the journey itself. Throughout the course of any collaborative endeavor, individuals come together, bringing their unique talents and perspectives to the table. They face challenges, overcome obstacles, and learn valuable lessons along the way. It is in these moments of reflection that true growth and mastery of leadership can be achieved.

Reflecting on the journey is an essential practice for anyone involved in teamwork, regardless of their role or setting. Whether you are a team leader, a team member, or an aspiring leader, taking the time to pause and evaluate the path you have traveled can provide invaluable insights and propel you forward.

One of the key benefits of reflection is the opportunity to acknowledge and celebrate achievements. By looking back on the journey, you can recognize the milestones you and your team have reached, no matter how big or small. Celebrating these accomplishments not only boosts morale but also reinforces the team's sense of purpose and motivation to continue moving forward.

Reflection also allows for an honest assessment of the team's performance. By examining the challenges faced and the strategies employed, you can identify areas of improvement and learn from past mistakes. This self-awareness is crucial for personal and team growth, as it enables individuals to refine their skills and develop more effective ways of working together.

Moreover, reflection cultivates a sense of gratitude and appreciation for the collective effort put forth by the team. It is an opportunity to recognize and acknowledge the contributions of each team member, fostering a culture of mutual respect and camaraderie. By expressing gratitude, team members feel valued and motivated to continue giving their best, ultimately strengthening the team's bond.

In addition to these benefits, reflecting on the journey also provides an occasion for personal growth and self-discovery. It allows individuals to evaluate their own strengths and weaknesses, enabling them to further develop their leadership abilities. By reflecting on past experiences, individuals can gain clarity on their values, goals, and aspirations, which in turn guides their future actions and decisions.

To truly master leadership in any setting, embracing the practice of reflecting on the journey is essential. It is through this process that teams can learn from their past, celebrate their achievements, and continuously improve. So, take a moment to pause, look back, and reflect on the journey. You may just discover new insights that will propel you and your team towards even greater success.

Applying Leadership Skills in Personal and Professional Life

Leadership is not limited to the professional realm; it is a skill that can be applied to all aspects of life. Whether you are leading a team at work or leading your own life, the principles of effective leadership remain the same. This subchapter explores the application of leadership skills in both personal and professional settings, emphasizing the importance of teamwork in achieving success.

In our personal lives, leadership skills can help us navigate through challenges, set goals, and make informed decisions. By honing our ability to communicate effectively, delegate tasks, and inspire others, we can create a positive and empowering environment for ourselves and those around us. Whether we are leading our families, social groups, or even just our own personal development, adopting a leadership mindset can help us achieve our desired outcomes.

Similarly, applying leadership skills in the professional realm is crucial for success in today's team-oriented workplace. Effective leaders not only possess the ability to motivate and guide their team members, but they also understand the importance of collaboration and cooperation. Teamwork is the cornerstone of any successful organization, and leaders play a vital role in fostering a culture of teamwork.

By utilizing their leadership skills, professionals can create a shared vision, set clear goals, and empower their team members to contribute their best. Strong leaders also understand the value of diversity and inclusion, recognizing that a diverse team brings a wealth of perspectives and ideas to the table. They encourage open communication, active listening, and mutual respect, creating an environment where everyone's voice is heard and valued.

In every setting, whether personal or professional, teamwork is essential for achieving success. Leaders who understand the power of collaboration and leverage their skills to foster effective teamwork can achieve remarkable results. By applying leadership skills, individuals can inspire and motivate others, build strong relationships, and create a sense of trust and loyalty within their teams.

In conclusion, leadership skills are not limited to the realm of business; they are applicable in all areas of life. By adopting a leadership mindset and implementing effective leadership practices, individuals can excel in their personal and professional lives. Teamwork triumphs when leaders understand the importance of collaboration, communication, and inclusion, creating an environment where everyone can thrive. Whether you are a team leader at work or striving to lead your own life, mastering leadership skills is essential for achieving success and making a positive impact on those around you.

Inspiring Others to Embrace Leadership and Teamwork

In today's fast-paced and interconnected world, the ability to work effectively as a team is crucial for success in any setting. Whether it's in the workplace, a sports team, or a community organization, teamwork is the foundation upon which great achievements are built. This subchapter aims to inspire and empower individuals to embrace leadership and teamwork, regardless of their background or experience.

Leadership is not limited to those in formal positions of authority; it is a mindset that anyone can adopt. By taking the initiative, setting a positive example, and motivating others, individuals can become leaders in their own right. This subchapter explores various strategies and techniques for inspiring others to embrace leadership, including leading by example, fostering open communication, and recognizing and nurturing the strengths of team members.

One of the most effective ways to inspire others to embrace teamwork is by creating a supportive and inclusive environment. This subchapter highlights the importance of building trust and fostering collaboration among team members. It discusses the role of effective communication in promoting teamwork, such as active listening, clear and concise instructions, and providing constructive feedback. Furthermore, it emphasizes the value of celebrating individual and team successes, as well as learning from failures, to foster a culture of continuous improvement.

The subchapter also delves into the power of storytelling in inspiring others to embrace leadership and teamwork. It explores how sharing personal experiences and anecdotes can engage and motivate team members, helping them to connect with the team's mission and goals on a deeper level.

Lastly, this subchapter addresses the challenges and barriers that individuals may face when trying to inspire others to embrace leadership and teamwork. It provides practical tips and strategies for overcoming these obstacles, such as promoting a growth mindset, encouraging creativity and innovation, and fostering a sense of belonging within the team.

Overall, this subchapter serves as a comprehensive guide for individuals who aspire to inspire others to embrace leadership and teamwork. It provides practical advice, real-life examples, and valuable insights to help readers cultivate the essential skills and mindset needed to succeed in any team setting.

www.ingramcontent.com/pod-product-compliance
Lightning Source LLC
LaVergne TN
LVHW052001060526
838201LV00059B/3782